How to make a Pizza

Written by Zoë Clarke
Photographs by Steve Lumb

Collins

6

Making a pizza

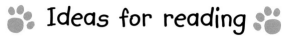 Ideas for reading

Written by Clare Dowdall BA(Ed), MA(Ed)
Lecturer and Primary Literacy Consultant

Learning objectives: use talk to organise, sequence and clarify thinking, ideas, feelings and events; extend their vocabulary, exploring the meaning and sounds of new words; show an understanding of how information can be found in non-fiction texts to answer questions about where, who, why and how

Curriculum links: Physical development: Recognise the importance of keeping healthy, and those things which contribute to this

Interest words: make, pizza

Resources: pizza recipes, whiteboard, paper and pens/ICT

Getting started

- Ask children to recall any cooking that they have done at home. Ask them to describe what they made and any ingredients that they needed.

- Look at the front and back covers together. Identify the food that has been cooked and the ingredients that were used to make it.

- Read the title and blurb to the children. Point to each word as it is read.

- Ask children if they like pizza and if so what toppings their favourites are.

Reading and responding

- Look at pp2–3 together. Discuss what is happening in the pictures, e.g. *the children are rolling out the dough with a rolling pin.* Support children to take turns to contribute to the discussion.

- Ask children to predict what needs to be prepared next for the pizza.

- As a group, turn to pp4–5. In pairs, ask children to talk about what is happening.

- Invite the children to share their ideas with the group. Support their contributions, using questioning to develop their vocabulary.